FUNNY SCHOOL JOKES

FOR TEACHERS AND STUDENTS

ZANE HOGAN

What did the daddy buffalo say to its son before it left for school?
"Bison."

Why did the skittles go to school?
Because they wanted to be Smarties!

What did the little elves have to do when they got home from school?
Gnome-work!

What's the fruitiest subject at school?
History, because it's full of dates!

What's a mathematician's favorite place to visit?
Times Square.

What is a balloon's least favorite school activity?
A pop quiz.

What do you call an algebra teacher who takes his vacations at the beach?
A tangent.

What are a cows favorite subjects in school?
Moosic, psycowolgy and cowculus!

What does Jack Frost like best about school?
Snow and tell.

What has a spine but, no bones?
A book!

Who's the biggest liar in school?
The Lie-brarian!

How does a math professor propose to his fiance?
With a polynomial ring!

What did the mathematician say when he lost his parrot?
"Where's my Polly-gon?"

Knock Knock!
Who's there?
Thayer!
Thayer who?
Thayer sorry and I won't tell teacher!

Why did the egg go to school?
To get "egg-u-cated"!

What do you call an ant who skips school?
A tru-ant!

Knock, knock.
Who's there?
Gladys.
Gladys, who?
Gladys the weekend—no homework!

Why did the bear eat the man reading a book
and not the man writing a book?
Because writers cramp and readers digest!

What do you learn at Santa's Helpers school?
The elf-a-bet!

Why don't you see giraffes in elementary school?
Because they're all in high school!

Son: I got in trouble today.
Mom: What did you do?
Son: The teacher moved my seat and said, "Sit here for the present time." So I waited a bit and then asked her when I would be receiving my gift!

Did you hear about the chemistry teacher who was reading the book about Helium?
He just couldn't put it down.

What is a snake's favorite subject?
Hiss-tory!

What does a monkey learn first in school?
The Apey-cees!

What do teachers drink at school?
Facul-Tea!

How do bees get to school?
On the school buzz!

Why did the model bring lipstick and eye shadow to school?
She had a make-up exam!

What did the dollar say to its math teacher?
"Does this make cents?"

Knock Knock.
Who's there?
Canoe.
Canoe who?
Canoe please help me with my homework?

Why did the freshman eat his homework?
Because his teacher said it was a piece of cake.

How did the cheese get hurt at school?
It was grated too hard.

What makes a Cyclops such an effective teacher?
He has only one pupil.

Why did the broom get a poor grade in school?
Because it was always sweeping during class!

Did you hear about the cross-eyed teacher
they fired last week?
She couldn't control her pupils!

What's the king of all school supplies?
The ruler.

What kind of math does a lumberjack need to
know?
Log-istics.

Why was Little Miss Muffet reading a map?
Because she lost her whey!

What did the math book say to the other
math book?
"I've got problems."

What did the principal say to the winning student?
"You're honor roll!"

Why don't you do arithmetic homework in the jungle?
Because if you add 4+4 you get ate.

What do moths study in school?
Mothematics!

What do you call a doctor that got C's all the way through med school?
Hopefully not your doctor!

What kind of math do birds like?
Owlgebra

Why did the music teacher need a ladder?
To reach the high notes.

What is the difference between a school teacher and a steam locomotive?
The school teacher tells you to spit out your gum, while the locomotive says "Choo Choo Choo!"

Student: Teacher, would you punish me for something I didn't do?
Teacher: Of course not.
Student: Good, because I didn't do my homework.

What kind of cake can you find in the school cafeteria?
Stomachache!

Why was the teacher wearing sunglasses to school?
She had bright students!

Why was school easier for cave people?
Because there was no history to study!

What did the fishing rod say to the boat?
Canoe help me with my homework?

Why did the students like their trigonometry teacher?
He never gave homework as-sin-ments.

What did the ghost teacher say to her class?
"Watch the board, and I'll go through it again."

Why did the principal bring Clam Chowder to school?
For the Soup-erintendent

Why are bad school grades like a shipwreck in the Arctic Ocean?
They're both below C level!

What kind of tree does a math teacher climb?
Geometry

What do you get if you cross a math teacher with a crab?
Snappy answers.

How do you know your math tutor is hungry?
He'll work for pi.

What kind of school do you go to if you're an ice cream man?
Sundae school.

A giant?
High school.

A surfer?
Boarding school

King Arthur?
Knight school.

Where do math teachers go on vacation?
Times Square.

Why are soccer players excellent at math?
They know how to use their heads.

In a Catholic's school's cafeteria, there was a bowl of apples on the table with a note that stated: "Take one only. God is watching." At the other end of the table, there was a pile of cookies with a note put there by one of the students: "Take all you want! God is watching the apples."

Why are some fish at the bottom of the ocean?
Because they dropped out of school!

What do you call a teacher who never passes gas at school?
A private tutor.

How are a teacher and a train alike?
They both have steam coming out of their ears!

Why did Captain Hook get suspended from school?
For playing hooky.

What's the difference between the Christmas alphabet and the ordinary alphabet?
The Christmas alphabet has Noel.

Where does a pawn go for higher education?
Knight school.

Why did the lamp go to school?
He wasn't very bright.

What did Sir Mix-A-Lot say in high school?
"Baby Got Backpack."

Why do you rarely find mathematicians spending time at the beach?
Because they have sine and cosine to get a tan and don't need the sun!

Why did the student give his teacher a PC?
The store was out of Apples!

Knock Knock.
Who's there?
Dewey!
Dewey who?
Dewey really have homework on the first day?

Why did the teacher marry the janitor?
Because he swept her off her feet!

What do you get if you add 52 apples and 423 pumpkins?
A middle school math problem!

Why did you eat your homework?
Because I don't have a dog.

What is a smart bird favorite type of math?
Owl-gebra

MOM: What did you do at school today?
Student: We did a guessing game.
MOM: But I thought you were having a math exam.
Student: We did!

Why was the teacher annoyed with the duck?
Because he wouldn't quit quackin' jokes!

What did the dog say to his classmate?
"Can I copy your homework, I ate mine."

What does a orangutan attorney study?
The Law of the jungle!

Teacher: Bobby, please use the word
"asbestos" in a sentence.
Bobby: "As best as I can tell, this homework
is a waste of time."

Why don't amoebas produce great
mathematicians?
Because they have to divide to multiply.

What happened to the Easter Bunny when he
misbehaved at school?
He was eggspelled!

Teacher: Class, we will have only half a day of school this morning.
Students: Hooray!
Teacher: We will have the other half this afternoon.

What do you call someone who can't stop doing math?
Add-icted!

What has given Mr. Bubbles nightmares since elementary school?
Pop quizzes!

Why did the school nurse bring a red pen to work?
In case she had to draw blood.

Where's the best place to hide in school?
Behind your math book—because there's
safety in numbers.

Did you hear about the boy who turned up to
school with only one glove? He said the
weather man said it's going to be cold but on
the other hand it might be warm!

What do you get when you combine classical
music with science fiction?
Bach to the Future!

What kind of music do teachers listen to?
Class-ical.

Where do elves go to school?
An elf-ementary school!

Student: Hey, Mom, I got a hundred in school today!
Mom: That's great.
Student: A 40 in Reading and a 60 in Math.

Why do magicians do so well in school?
They're good at trick questions.

How many geometry teachers does it take to replace a light bulb?
None. They can't do it, but they can prove that it can be done.

How does a mathematician scold her children?
"If I've told you n times, I've told you n+1 times..."

What do you call a geometry teacher who studies magic?
A mathemagician!

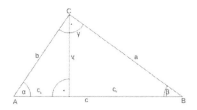

Why wasn't the geometry teacher at school?
Because she sprained her angle!

Where do belly buttons go to school?
The Navel Academy!

What do history teachers talk about on dates?
The good old days!

What is an English teacher's favorite breakfast?
A synonym roll!

Why did Tommy bring her skunk to school?
For show-and-smell!

What happened to the plant in math class?
It grew square roots.

What is the math teacher's favorite dessert?
Pi.

What did the teacher say when the horse
walked into her class?
"Why the long face?"

What is a runner's favorite subject in school?
Jog-raphy!

If the pilgrims came on the Mayflower than what did the teachers come on?
The scholar ships.

What is the first thing that bats learn at school?
The alpha-bat.

What did the mathematician's parrot say?
A poly "no meal"

Why do fish swim in schools?
Because they can't walk!

What do chickens call a school test? Eggs-amination!

Daughter: I can't go to school today. I don't
Dad: Where don't you feel well?
Daughter: In school!

What do you call friends who love math?
Algebros.

What do you call the period of time following
algebra?
The aftermath.

Why was the candle failing school?
It just wasn't that bright!

What's a teacher's favorite nation?
Expla-nation.

Did you hear about the zombie who was
expelled from school?
He kept buttering up his teacher!

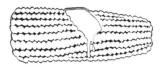

What does a lumberjack have in common
with a preschooler?

What do they teach in witching school?
Spell-ing.

I asked my teacher about shaving, but he
said, "You must razor hand first"

Principal: I hear you missed the first day
back to school.
Student: Yes, but I didn't miss it very much!

Knock Knock.
Who's there?
Stopwatch!
Stopwatch who?
Stopwatch your doing and pay attention to the math teacher!

What does corn say after failing a test at school?
"Aw, shucks!"

Knock Knock.
Who's there?
Howl.
Howl who?
Howl we finish our homework on time?

Why did the teacher jump into the lake?
She wanted to test the water!

Knock Knock.Who's there?
Carson.
Carson who?
Carson in school is not allowed!

What do you get when you complete science class?
A graduated cylinder.

Why was the Calculus teacher bad at baseball?
He was better at fitting curves than hitting them.

Knock Knock.Who's there?
Cindy?
Cindy who?
I'm Cindy you to the principal's office!

What do chickens study in school?
Eggonomics.

What is a soda's favorite school subject?
Fizz ed.

What would you get if you crossed a vampire
and a teacher?
Bood tests!

Teacher: Did you skip school yesterday and
go to the ball game? Student:
No, ma'am, and I've got the movie ticket stub
to prove it!

What kind of monkey flies to school?
A hot air baboon.

Dad: Steven, did you do your homework?
Son: No, sir. I'm saving it for a brainy day.

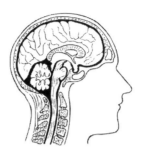

Mom: "What did you learn today?"
Student: "Not enough. They said I have to go back tomorrow."

Tongue Twisters

A box of biscuits, a batch of mixed biscuits

A skunk sat on a stump and thunk the stump stunk,
but the stump thunk the skunk stunk.

Principal Piper picked a pack of purple papers.
Did Principal Piper pick a pack of purple papers?
If Principal Piper picked a pack of purple papers,
where's the pack of purple papers Principal Piper
picked?

Red lorry, yellow lorry, red lorry, yellow lorry.

A big black bug bit a big black bear,
made the big black bear bleed blood.

Mrs. Smith's Fish Sauce Shop.

Shy Shelly says she shall sew sheets.

Three free throws.
Which wristwatches are Swiss wristwatches?

The myth of Miss Muffet.

Friendly Frank flips fine flapjacks.

Gertie's great-grandma grew aghast at Gertie's grammar.

Fat frogs flying past fast.

Greek grapes.

We surely shall see the sun shine soon.

Sly Sam slurps Sally's soup.

Three gray geese in the green grass grazing.
Gray were the geese and green was the grass.

Crisp crusts crackle crunchily.

Give papa a cup of proper coffee in a copper coffee
cup.

Six shimmering sharks sharply striking shins.

Betty and Bob brought back blue balloons from the
big bazaar.

While we were walking, we were watching window washers
wash Washington's windows with warm washing water.

The crow flew over the river
with a lump of raw liver.

Preshrunk silk shirts

Cedar shingles should be shaved and saved.

Are our oars oak?

Kris Kringle carefully crunched on candy canes.

Please pay promptly.

What time does the wristwatch strap shop shut?

Freshly-fried flying fish.

Made in the USA
San Bernardino, CA
19 May 2019